A Trip to Mini Town

By JoAnne Nelson • Pictures by Ethel Gold

MODERN CURRICULUM PRESS

PROJECT DIRECTOR: Judith E. Nayer
COVER DESIGN: Elaine A. Groth

Published by Modern Curriculum Press

Modern Curriculum Press, Inc.
A division of Simon & Schuster
13900 Prospect Road, Cleveland, Ohio 44136

ISBN 0-8136-4335-X (STY PK)   ISBN 0-8136-4331-7 (BK)

10 9 8 7 6 5 4 3 2   94 93 92 91

I'm on my way to Mini Town.
I just can't wait to get there.
There'll be mini people all around.
I wonder if I'll fit there.

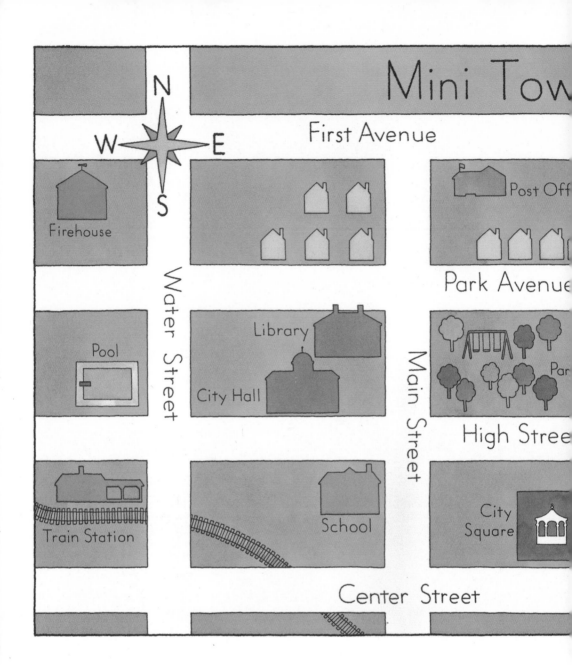

A mini map and map key
will help me get around.
I'll follow the directions
as I go through Mini Town.

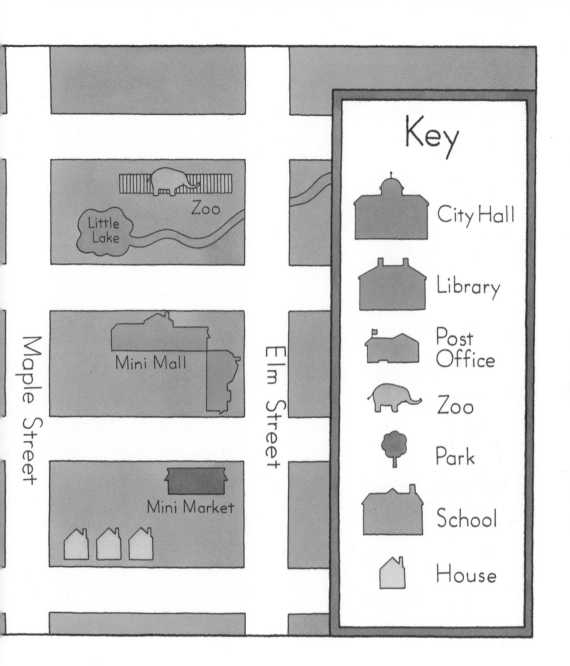

The map key has small pictures
for the park, the school, the zoo,
for City Hall, the library,
and the new post office, too.

Main Street goes north and south.
High Street goes east and west.
The city pool's on Water Street.
I think I'll like it best.

I started out at City Hall.
The mayor was at work.
I met the city council,
and then the city clerk.

The Mini Town Library
was the next stop on my way.
I passed the park and playground
where the mini children play.

I walked north past mini houses.
I saw the new post office, too.
I walked east along First Avenue
until I reached the zoo.

Then I walked south on Elm Street.
I passed the Mini Mall.
I found the Mini Market—
I wasn't lost at all.

I headed west on Center Street
to find the City Square.
A band was playing music.
All the mini folks were there.

I went to the next corner,
and then I took a right.
I passed the school on Main Street,
but the pool was not in sight.

I checked my map and map key.
I turned and headed west.
I finally found the Mini Pool.
Now I KNOW I like it best!

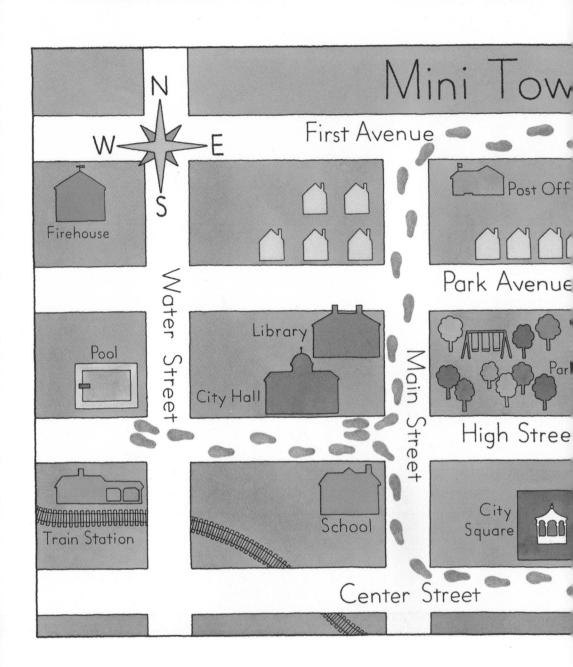

You can take a trip through Mini Town.
You can trace the path I took.
Just follow all the footsteps
while you take another look.

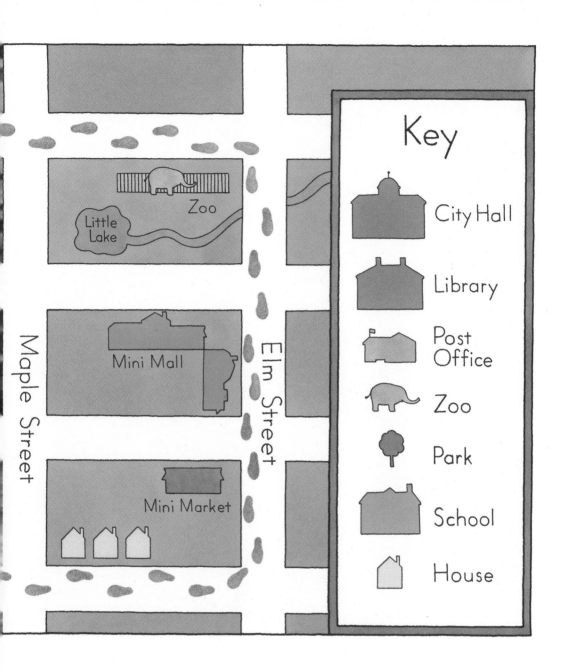

The mini map and map key
will help you get around.
I hope you like your travels
as you go through Mini Town!

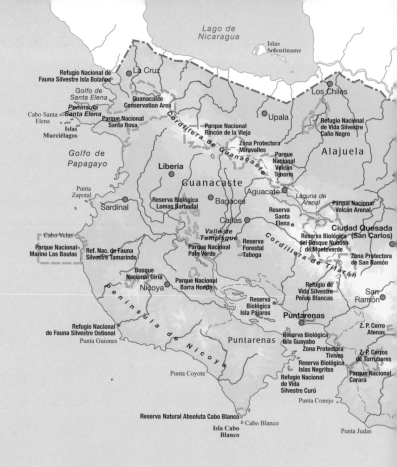

Lago de Nicaragua

Islas Solentiname

Refugio Nacional de Fauna Silvestre Isla Bolaños

La Cruz

Los Chiles

Golfo de Santa Elena

Guanacaste Conservation Area

Upala

Refugio Nacional de Vida Silvestre Caño Negro

Cabo Santa Elena

Península Santa Elena

Parque Nacional Santa Rosa

Parque Nacional Rincón de la Vieja

Islas Murciélagos

Zona Protectora Miravalles

Parque Nacional Volcán Tenorio

Alajuela

Golfo de Papagayo

Liberia

Guanacaste

Aguacate

Laguna de Arenal

Parque Nacional Volcán Arenal

Punta Zapotal

Reserva Biológica Lomas Barbudal

Bagaces

Reserva Santa Elena

Sardinal

Cañas

Ciudad Quesada (San Carlos)

Cabo Velas

Valle de Tempisque

Reserva Forestal Taboga

Reserva Biológica del Bosque Nuboso de Monteverde

Parque Nacional Marino Las Baulas

Ref. Nac. de Fauna Silvestre Tamarindo

Parque Nacional Palo Verde

Zona Protectora de San Ramón

Bosque Nacional Diriá

Parque Nacional Barra Honda

Refugio de Vida Silvestre Peñas Blancas

San Ramón

Nicoya

Reserva Biológica Isla Pájaros

Puntarenas

Z. P. Cerro Atenas

Refugio Nacional de Fauna Silvestre Ostional

Punta Guiones

Puntarenas

Reserva Biológica Isla Guayabo

Zona Protectora Tivives

Z. P. Cerros de Turrubares

Reserva Biológica Islas Negritos

Parque Nacional Carara

Punta Coyote

Refugio Nacional de Vida Silvestre Curú

Punta Conejo

Reserva Natural Absoluta Cabo Blanco

Cabo Blanco

Isla Cabo Blanco

Punta Judas

PACIFIC OCEAN

Isla del Coco

0   2 km
0   2 miles

Punta Agujas

Isla Manuelita

Isla Pájara

Bahía Chatham

Bahía Wafer

Cabo Barreto

Parque Nacional Isla del Coco

Cerro Yglesias 634

Cerro Jesús Jiménez 430

Cabo Atrevida

Cabo Lionel

Isla Muela

Cabo Dampier